My Child's Swimming Logbook

© All content is Copyright Lizzie Zawinski @weeburstofawesome. Happy Swimming! :)

Welcome To Your Wild Swimming Logbook!

Your Wild Swimming experiences are special. There is absolutely no doubt about that. But what exactly is it that makes each of your Wild Swimming experience so wonderful?

The thrill of swimming outside under the sky? Being surrounded by natural beauty? The incredible supportive camaraderie between people from very different walks of life? Slipping into the chill and swimming? Laughter as you enter the water with your friends? Or the giggles while you get changed at the water's edge afterwards? The shared jokes and experiences that have bonded you, creating memories that you will cherish forever?

It may be all of the above for some swims, or one thing that shines out for a particular dip. Whatever it is, this book is here to help you capture it.

Looking back over your swims and dips is guaranteed to bring a smile to your face and remind you of the special nuances of each individual swim.

This logbook was designed for those of us who enter the water to challenge only ourselves, to enjoy the moment, not to compete with anybody else or chase times.
We are here for the experience, the friendship, and that special feeling of accomplishment after each outdoor dip that we can't quite completely explain to anyone who hasn't tried it. The addictive little thill that makes us enthuse about the moments we spend in the wild water, or next to it with our fellow swimmers. It's what makes us try to persuade anyone we know that they should come and experience the magic too, even if it sounds a bit bonkers!

If you are one of us you will know exactly what I am describing. You are probably nodding as you remember moments of laughter and gasping shrieks as the water hits sensitive parts of the body. Times when the sun sparkles on the water and you can't imagine wanting to be anywhere else. The sense of calm fulfilment as you head back to your towel and start to peel off your wet swimwear. Enjoying true friendship as bonds are strengthened with floods of words spoken over steaming hot cups and plates of cake.

It is a very special world to be part of, this Wild Swimming malarky. Here's to lots of adventures in and out of the water; stay safe and don't forget to have fun!

Some notes on using your logbook...

Date & Location are obvious (I hope!)

Date:

    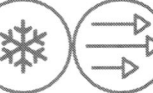

Location:

Weather symbols can be coloured in (if that's your type of thing)

Space to record Air & Water Temperature

Who Was There:

Fairly obvious right? There is also plenty of space to get creative adding your group's personalities and characteristics with beards, notes on silly reactions or drawing the new swimsuit patterns spotted today!

(Sometimes there are a LOT of people there!)

It can be helpful to keep a track of how long you were in the water, but paying attention to your body is the best timing device. Every day you bring a different energy level to the water.

Time Spent In The Water:

The Best Part:

What did YOU like best about today?

Sometimes the tiny things are what makes it an utterly magical swim :)

Afterwards:

Was there a new cake flavour?

How did you FEEL?
Elated? Content?
Did you warm up ok?

What was the hot beverage of choice today?

Remember your bright swim hat, tow-float and other warming essentials!

Stay Safe

FLOAT

Don't forget your your towel! ← *Is there anything worse?!*

Date:

Location:

Who Was There:

Time Spent In The Water:

The Best Part:

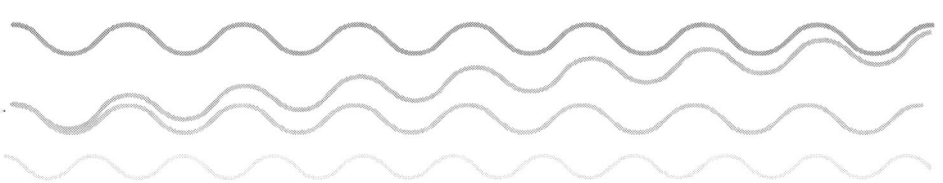

Afterwards:

Don't forget your your towel!

Date:

Location:
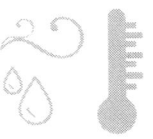

Who Was There:

Time Spent In The Water:

The Best Part:

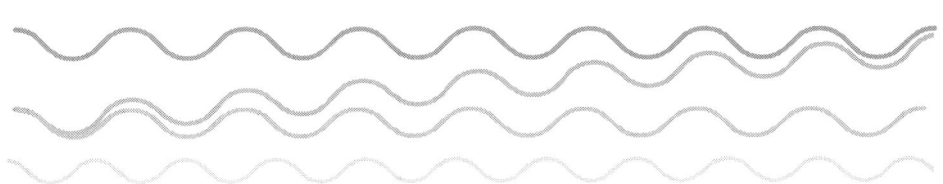

Afterwards:

Stay Safe

Don't forget your your towel!

Date: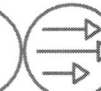

Location:

~~~~~~~~~~~~~~~~~~~~~~~~~~~~

Who Was There:

Time Spent In The Water:

~~~~~~~~~~~~~~~~~~~~~~~~~~~~

The Best Part:

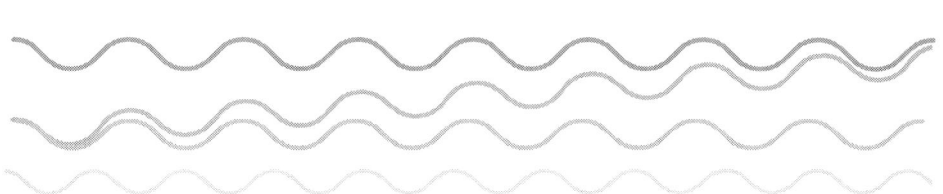

Afterwards:

Stay Safe

Don't forget your your towel!

Date: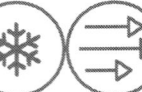

Location:

Who Was There:

Time Spent In The Water:

The Best Part:

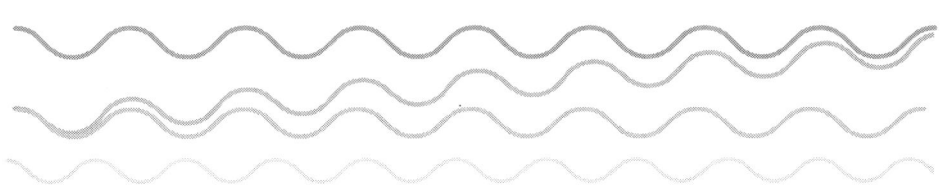

Afterwards:

Don't forget your your towel!

Date:

Location:

Who Was There:

Time Spent In The Water:

The Best Part:

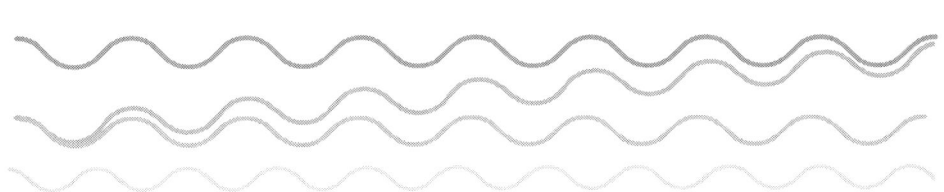

Afterwards:

Stay Safe

Don't forget your your towel!

Date:

Location:

Who Was There:

Time Spent In The Water:

The Best Part:

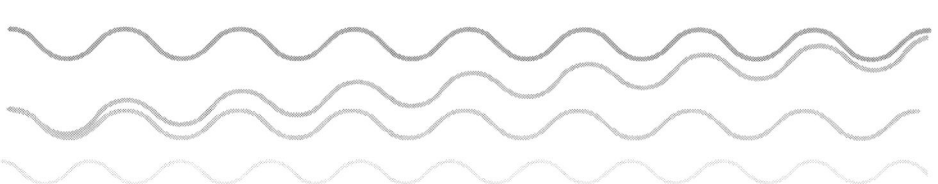

Afterwards:

Stay Safe

FLOAT

Don't forget your your towel!

Date:

Location: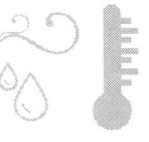

Who Was There:

Time Spent In The Water:

The Best Part:

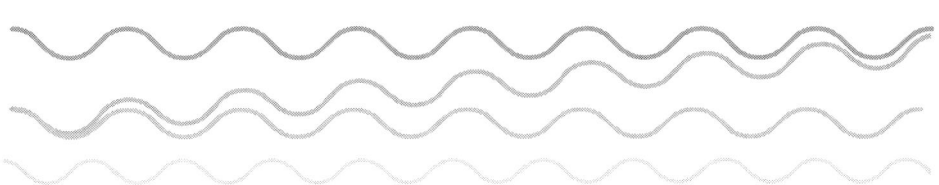

Afterwards:

Stay Safe

Don't forget your your towel!

Date:

Location:

Who Was There:

Time Spent In The Water:

The Best Part:

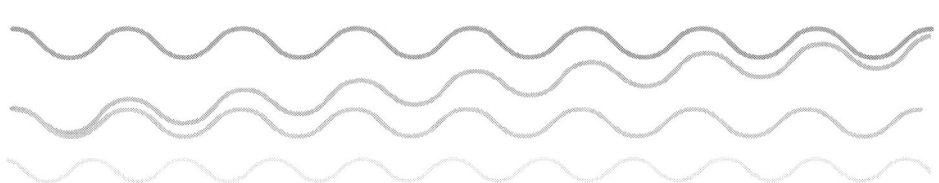

Afterwards:

Don't forget your your towel!

Date:

Location:

Who Was There:

Time Spent In The Water:

The Best Part:

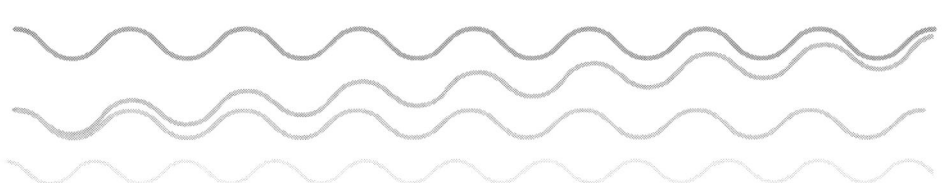

Afterwards:

Don't forget your your towel!

Date:

Location:

Who Was There:

Time Spent In The Water:

The Best Part:

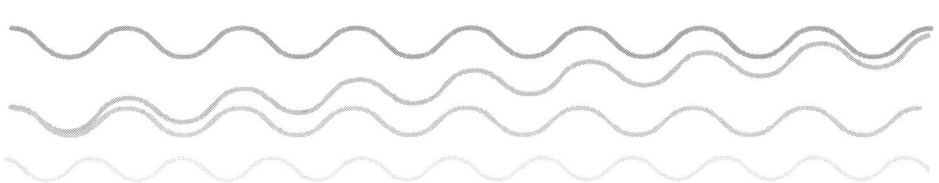

Afterwards:

Stay Safe

Don't forget your your towel!

Date:

Location:

Who Was There:

Time Spent In The Water:

The Best Part:

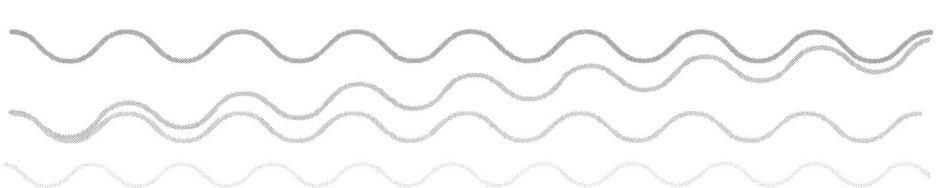

Afterwards:

Stay Safe

FLOAT

Don't forget your your towel!

Date:

Location:

Who Was There:

Time Spent In The Water:

The Best Part:

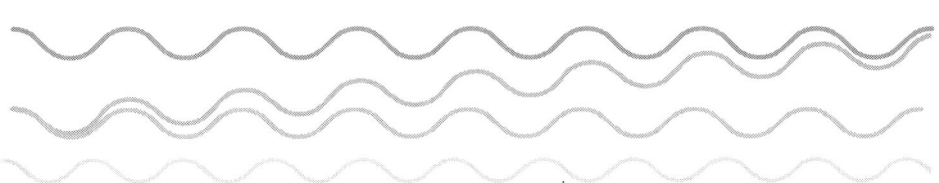

Afterwards:

Stay Safe

Don't forget your your towel!

Date:

Location:

Who Was There:

Time Spent In The Water:

The Best Part:

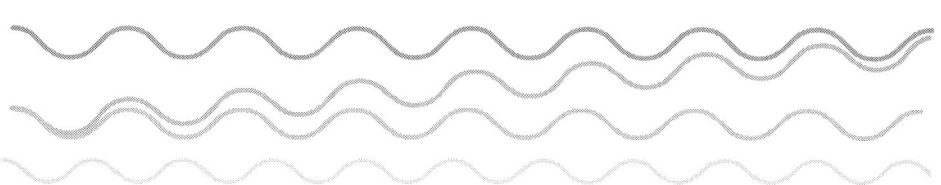

Afterwards:

Don't forget your your towel!

Date:

Location:

Who Was There:

Time Spent In The Water:

The Best Part:

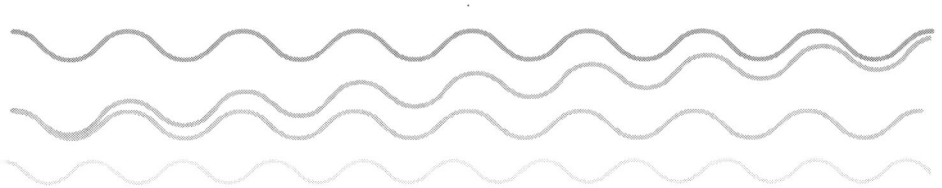

Afterwards:

Don't forget your your towel!

Date:

Location:

Who Was There:

Time Spent In The Water:

The Best Part:

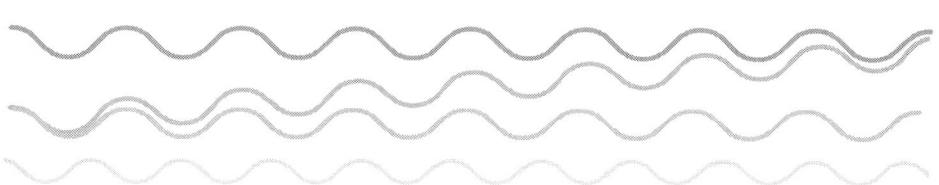

Afterwards:

Don't forget your your towel!

Date:

Location: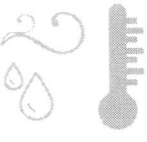

Who Was There:

Time Spent In The Water:

The Best Part:

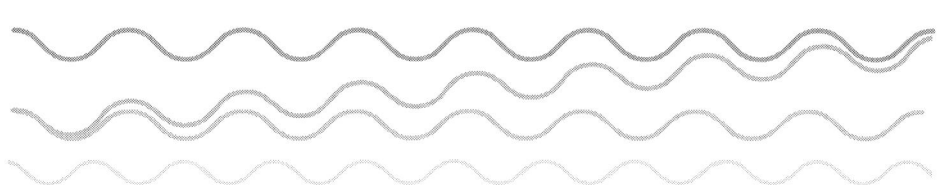

Afterwards:

Stay Safe

Don't forget your your towel!

Date:

Location:

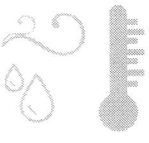

Who Was There:

Time Spent In The Water:

The Best Part:

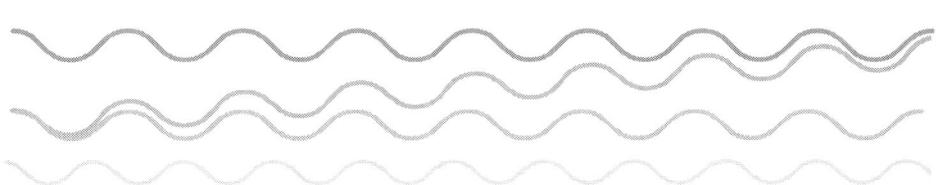

Afterwards:

Don't forget your your towel!

Date:

Location: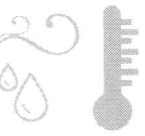

Who Was There:

Time Spent In The Water:

The Best Part:

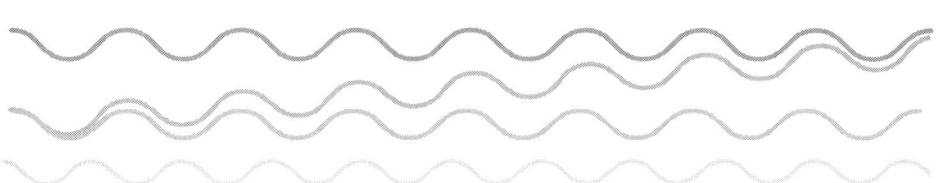

Afterwards:

Don't forget your your towel!

Date:

Location:

Who Was There:

Time Spent In The Water:

The Best Part:

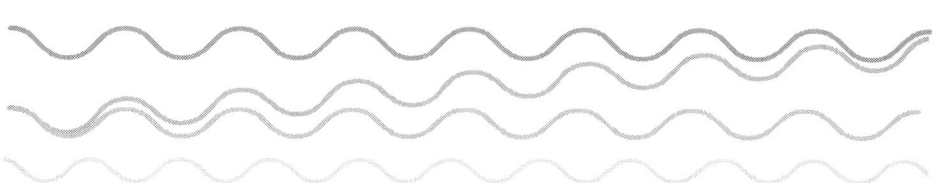

Afterwards:

Stay Safe

Don't forget your your towel!

Date:

Location:

Who Was There:

Time Spent In The Water:

The Best Part:

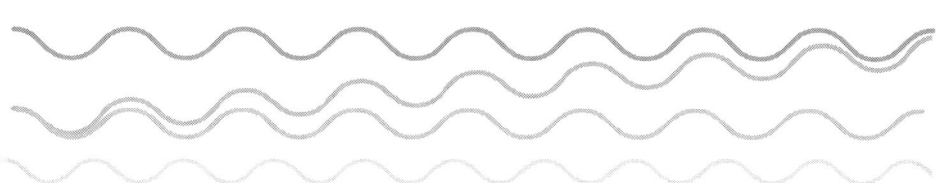

Afterwards:

Stay Safe

Don't forget your your towel!

Date:

Location:

Who Was There:

Time Spent In The Water:

The Best Part:

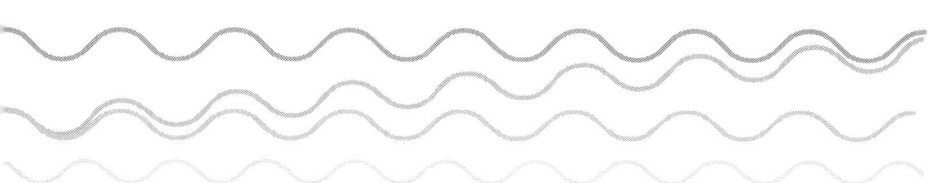

Afterwards:

Stay Safe

FLOAT

Don't forget your your towel!

Date:

Location:

Who Was There:

Time Spent In The Water:

The Best Part:

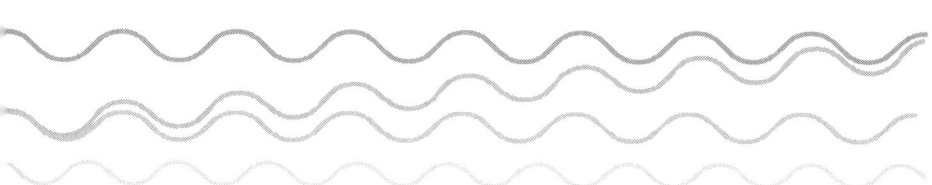

Afterwards:

Don't forget your your towel!

Date:

Location:

Who Was There:

Time Spent In The Water:

The Best Part:

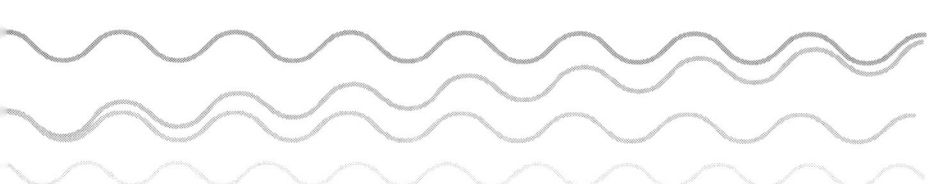

Afterwards:

Stay Safe

Don't forget your your towel!

Date:

Location:

Who Was There:

Time Spent In The Water:

The Best Part:

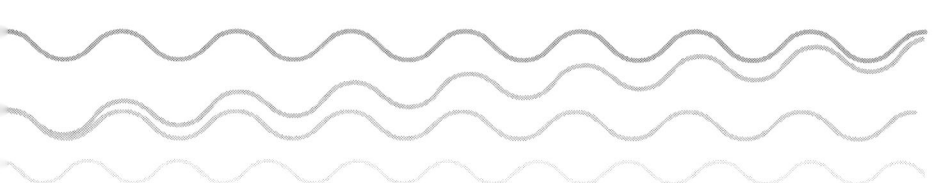

Afterwards:

Don't forget your your towel!

Date:

Location:

Who Was There:

Time Spent In The Water:

The Best Part:

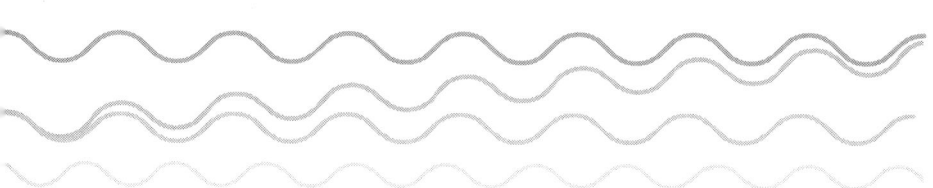

Afterwards:

Don't forget your your towel!

Date:

Location:

Who Was There:

Time Spent In The Water:

The Best Part:

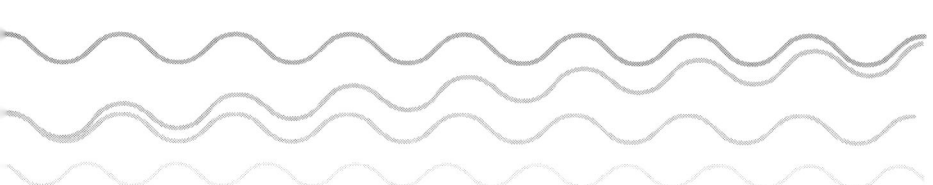

Afterwards:

Don't forget your your towel!

Date:

Location:

Who Was There:

Time Spent In The Water:

The Best Part:

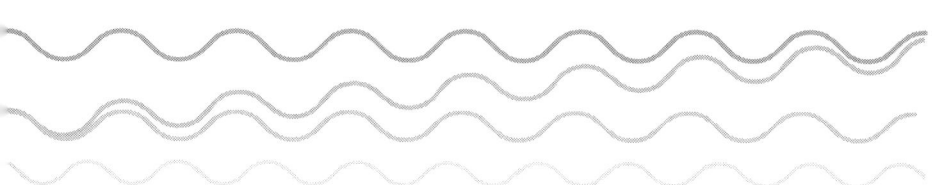

Afterwards:

Don't forget your your towel!

Date:

Location:

Who Was There:

Time Spent In The Water:

The Best Part:

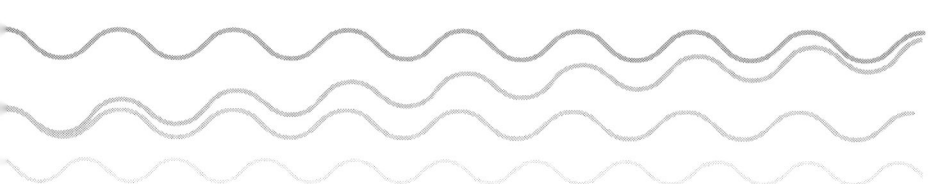

Afterwards:

Stay Safe

Don't forget your your towel!

Date:

Location:

Who Was There:

Time Spent In The Water:

The Best Part:

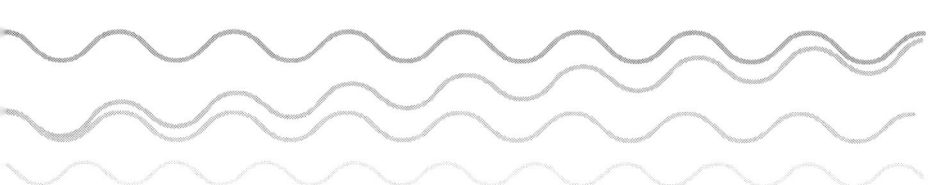

Afterwards:

Don't forget your your towel!

Date:

Location:

Who Was There:

Time Spent In The Water:

The Best Part:

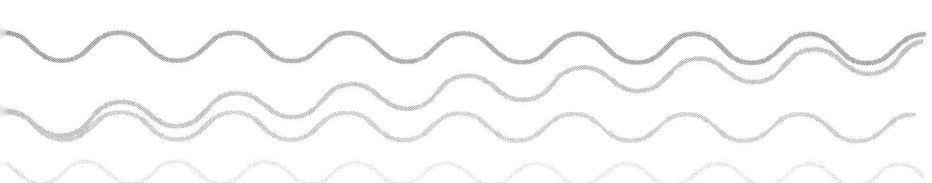

Afterwards:

Stay Safe

Don't forget your your towel!

Date:

Location:

Who Was There:

Time Spent In The Water:

The Best Part:

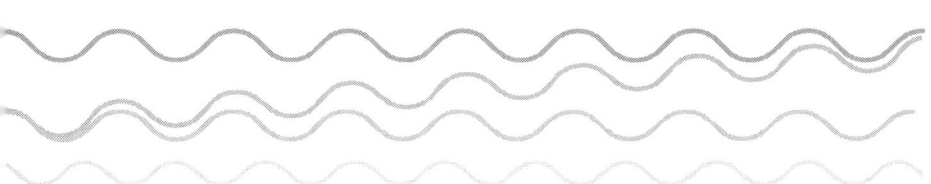

Afterwards:

Stay Safe

Don't forget your your towel!

Date:

Location:

Who Was There:

Time Spent In The Water:

The Best Part:

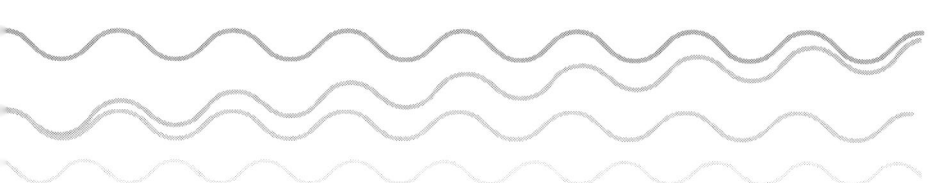

Afterwards:

Stay Safe

Don't forget your your towel!

Date:

Location:

Who Was There:

Time Spent In The Water:

The Best Part:

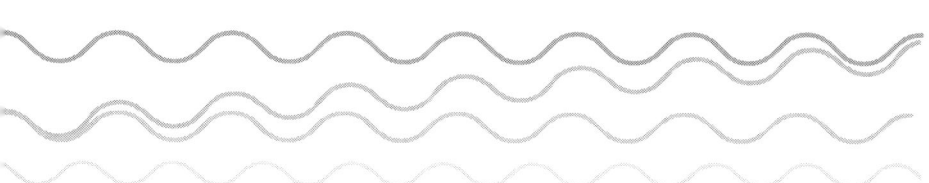

Afterwards:

Stay Safe

Don't forget your your towel!

Date:

Location:

Who Was There:

Time Spent In The Water:

The Best Part:

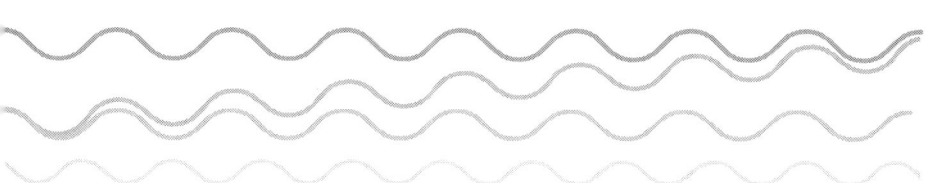

Afterwards:

Stay Safe

Don't forget your your towel!

Date:

Location:

Who Was There:

Time Spent In The Water:

The Best Part:

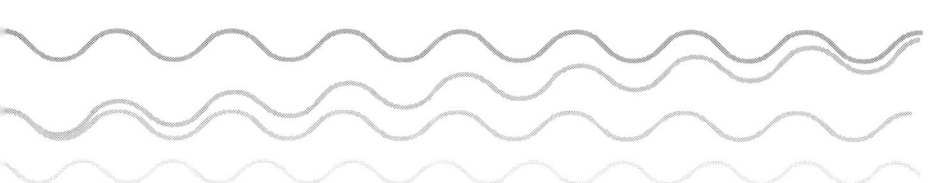

Afterwards:

Don't forget your your towel!

Date:

Location:

Who Was There:

Time Spent In The Water:

The Best Part:

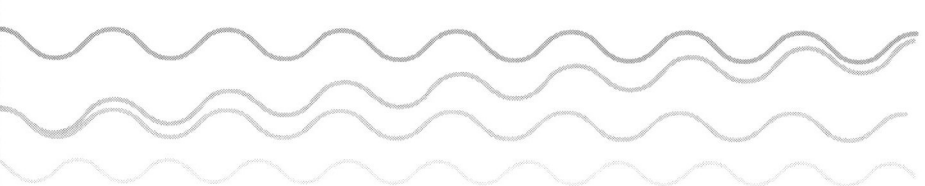

Afterwards:

Don't forget your your towel!

Date:

Location:

Who Was There:

Time Spent In The Water:

The Best Part:

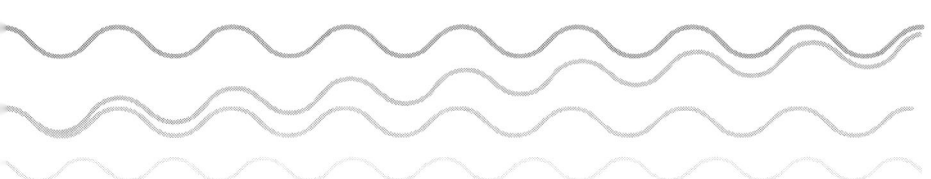

Afterwards:

Don't forget your your towel!

Date:

Location:

Who Was There:

Time Spent In The Water:

The Best Part:

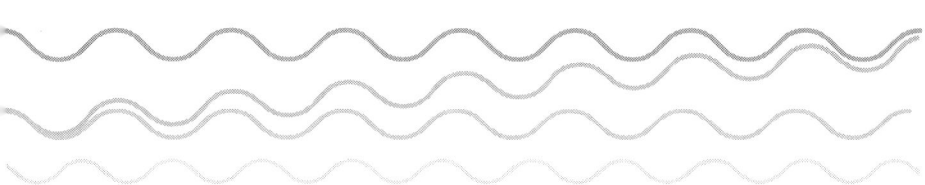

Afterwards:

Don't forget your your towel!

Date:

Location:

Who Was There:

Time Spent In The Water:

The Best Part:

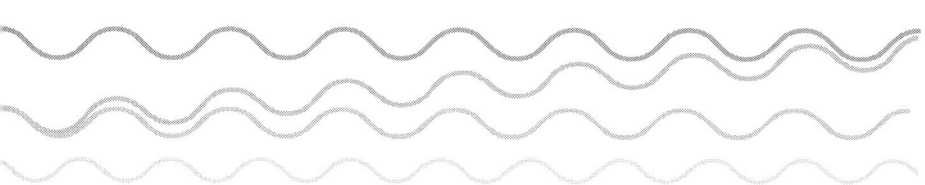

Afterwards:

Stay Safe

Don't forget your your towel!

Date:

Location:

Who Was There:

Time Spent In The Water:

The Best Part:

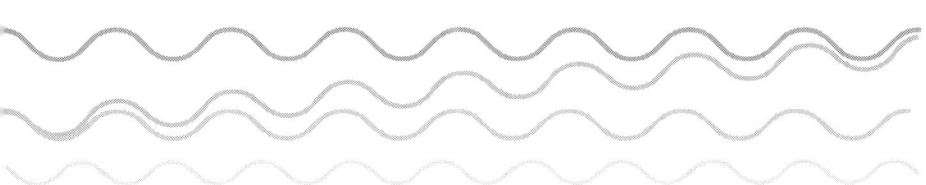

Afterwards:

Stay Safe

Don't forget your your towel!

Date:

Location:

Who Was There:

Time Spent In The Water:

The Best Part:

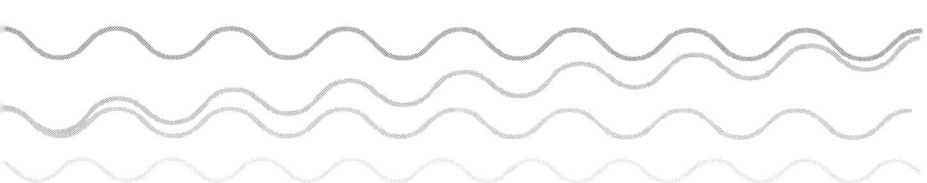

Afterwards:

Don't forget your your towel!

Date:

Location:

Who Was There:

Time Spent In The Water:

The Best Part:

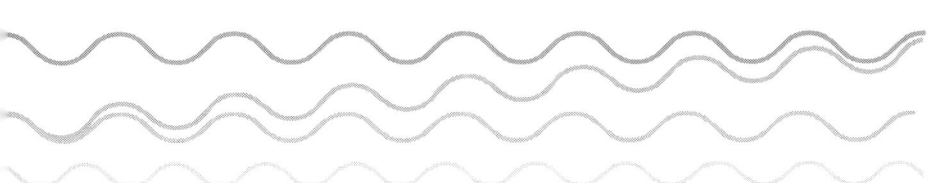

Afterwards:

Stay Safe

Don't forget your your towel!

Here's to lots more wild swimming adventures full of laughter, and cake!

© All content is Copyright Lizzie Zawinski @weeburstofawesome. Happy Swimming! :)

Printed in Great Britain
by Amazon